A Personal Tour of
A SHAKER VILLAGE

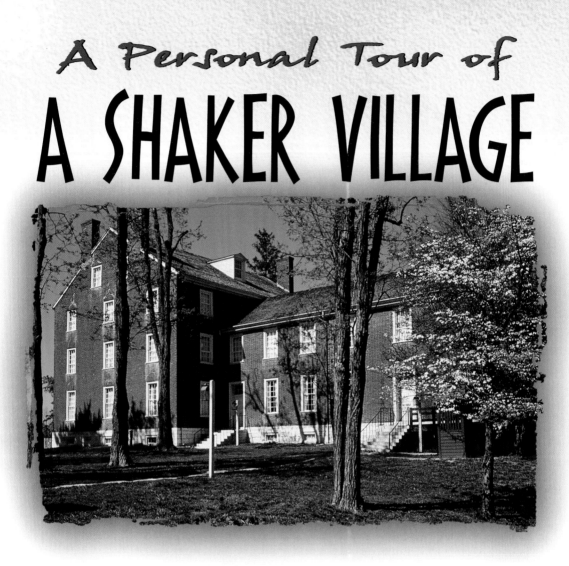

BY MICHAEL CAPEK

LERNER PUBLICATIONS COMPANY • MINNEAPOLIS

Cover: *In the Broom Maker's Shop, a volunteer interpreter makes brooms the same way Shakers made them in the 1800s.*
Title page: *Shakers lived, slept, and ate their meals in dormitory-like buildings, such as the red brick East Family Dwelling.*

Thanks to Larrie Curry, Museum Director at Pleasant Hill, for her kindness and invaluable assistance during the research of this book. Thanks, as well, to Susan Hughes, Randy Folger, and all the craftspeople, experts, and interpreters at Pleasant Hill who keep the spirit burning bright.

For my mother. She put her "hands to work and her heart to God."

Copyright © 2001 by Michael Capek

Lerner Publications Company
A division of Lerner Publishing Group
241 First Avenue North
Minneapolis, MN 55401 U.S.A.

Website address: www.lernerbooks.com

LIBRARY OF CONGRESS CATALOGING-IN-PUBLICATIONS DATA

Capek, Michael.
  A personal tour of a Shaker village / by Michael Capek.
    p. cm. — (How it was)
  Includes index.
    ISBN 0-8225-3584-X (lib. bdg. : alk. paper)
    1. Shakers—Kentucky—Pleasant Hill—Juvenile literature. 2. Pleasant Hill (Ky.)—Juvenile literature. [1. Shakers. 2. Pleasant Hill (Ky.)] I. Title. II. How it was (Minneapolis, Minn.)
  BX9768.P6 C37 2001
  289'.8'09769485—dc21   00-009316

Manufactured in the United States of America
1 2 3 4 5 6 – JR – 06 05 04 03 02 01

Contents

Introduction   5

With Benjamin Dunlavy   13

With Patsy Roberts Williamson   23

With Hortensia Hooser   31

With John Shain   39

With a Visitor   49

Afterword   57

Glossary and Pronunciation Guide   61

Further Reading and Touring Information   62

Index   63

About the Author   64

During Shaker religious services, men and women marched, danced, and sang.

At Manchester, in England,
This holy fire began . . . .

—from *Millennial Praises, Part II,* 1813

Introduction

The Shakers, a religious group, formed in England near Manchester during the 1740s. The Shakers were a handful of dissenters (Christians dissatisfied with the way worship was carried out in both Protestant and Catholic churches of the time). Officially known as the United Society of Believers in Christ's Second Appearing, the group met in members' homes to worship. The Believers often shook, shouted, danced, and sang during their worship. Outsiders mocked them with the name "Shakers," but the Believers soon adopted the nickname. After all, it described them perfectly.

In 1758 a young woman named Ann Lees joined the Society. Ann was broken from overwork in the workshops of Manchester, England. She mourned the deaths of her four children. Ann came to the Shakers seeking comfort, but soon she led the worship. The Believers called her

"Mother Ann." Mother Ann told Shakers that she had visions. She seemed to almost glow as she said that God had spoken to her.

Mother Ann told the Believers that they should no longer live as husband and wife. Ann explained that God was the father and people were his children. This meant that all men and women were brothers and sisters, who could not marry or have children. She went on to say that everyone was equal in the eyes of God—men and women, black and white, rich and poor. She also said that the Believers should try to live pure, clean lives. They should also separate from **the world** in every way. This meant that they should form communities where only Shakers lived.

Ann Lees' most amazing revelation was that God is both male and female. "I am Ann, the Word," she said. Other Shakers weren't sure what she meant. Many assumed she meant that she represented the second coming of Jesus.

Membership increased, and the group's activities became more public. Many people found the Shaker message strange and contrary to their own beliefs. People who disagreed with the Shakers' beliefs formed mobs that howled outside Shaker meeting places. Mother Ann was arrested several times for disturbing the peace.

In 1774 Mother Ann informed the Shakers that God had told them to go to America. A small group of Shakers crossed the Atlantic to settle in Niskeyuna, New York (modern-day Watervliet). The group began building a village and farming the land.

Shakers built villages in rural areas surrounded by pastures, streams, and trees. The villages were composed of several buildings for working and worshiping.

The Shakers were pacifists, people who will not fight or commit any violent acts. Because of this, Shakers refused to fight in the Revolutionary War (1775–1783). Both sides labeled the Shakers as traitors. Finally, the British threw Mother Ann into prison for a year. When the British governor of New York finally realized Mother Ann's motives were spiritual and not political, the governor released her. But violence against Shakers continued. Some people threw stones at Mother Ann and other Shaker leaders when they tried to preach the Shaker gospel.

In 1784 Mother Ann died at the age of 48. Two **elders** (leaders), James Whittaker and Joseph Meacham, took control of the Society. Instead of being weakened by the loss of Mother Ann, new members flocked to the Believers. Everybody was welcome—men, women, families, orphans, rich landowners, poor folk, former slaves,

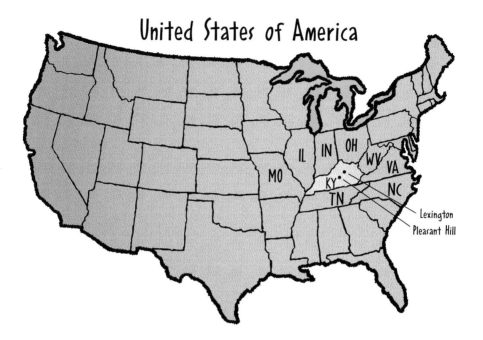

United States of America

Lexington
Pleasant Hill

and even former slaveowners. Shakers built a village at New Lebanon, New York. By 1794 Shakers had founded eleven communities in New York, Maine, New Hampshire, Connecticut, and Massachusetts. Eventually, eighteen major Shaker communities would be organized in eight states, with six smaller ones in Florida and Indiana.

In 1805 Shaker missionaries (people who undertake religious assignments) moved into Ohio and Kentucky to found new villages. Six year later, in 1811, a devout group of Believers organized a community on gently rolling farmland in the Bluegrass region of central Kentucky, near the Kentucky River. The site lay west of the town of Lexington and south of Louisville. The Believers called the village Pleasant Hill.

Over the next forty years, Shakers bought land and

built dwellings, shops, and mills. They constructed a meetinghouse modeled on the one in Niskeyuna, New York. By 1850 Pleasant Hill sprawled across some 4,400 acres. The village was divided into East, West, Center, North, and Northeast groups, called **families.** Each family had about one hundred members, and each was made up of both men and women. Each family had its own barns, shops, gardens, fields, wash house, and dwelling house. Men, women, and children (who had been born before joining the Shaker community) made up the families, but men and women slept in separate rooms. (If a family from the outside world joined the Shakers, husbands, wives, and children—who had been born before they joined the Shakers—separated to join new families.)

Each family had four elders: two men and two women. Elders coordinated work and resources. Elders also

Many Shakers slept and ate in the large Centre Family Dwelling. The Meeting House (right) *was across the main street from the Centre Family Dwelling.*

Ministers led solitary lives of quiet leadership and intense devotion. Because of the awesome responsibility they carried, the two male and two female ministers never mingled or socialized with other villagers. That way, friendships or petty grudges couldn't affect their decisions. They ate in a separate dining room and worked in separate shops.

tended the spiritual needs of their families. Elders appointed deacons and deaconesses to oversee the smaller details of life. Pleasant Hill had a kitchen deaconess, a mechanical deacon, a garden deaconess, and a farm deacon, to name a few. Trustees handled dealings with the outside world. They dealt with real estate, property, contracts, and other legal matters.

The **ministry** oversaw everything at Pleasant Hill. Specially chosen by the headquarters in New York for their

Male and female Shakers sat opposite each other at meetings.

faith, strength, judgment, and humility, these men and women guided the whole village. They made the final decisions about everything that happened at Pleasant Hill. They decided what crops to plant and when to plant them. The ministry determined what the village's workshops should make. They appointed the salespeople who would sell goods and produce to members of the world. The ministry decided how to spend the money the salespeople earned. The ministry also elected the trustees, elders, and deacons.

Although they shared the same dwelling houses, men and women lived separate lives. Men lived on the east side of a house, women on the west. They ate their meals on opposite sides of the dining room. They worked in separate sisters' or brothers' shops. Men

> **T**he Shakers led lives of seclusion from people who weren't Believers. The Shakers called these folks **"the world's people."** That's the way they wanted it—most of the time. Office trustees were appointed to greet visitors and to conduct business with the non-Shaker world. That way, most of the people in the village were shielded from contact with the world.

and women had evening discussions in the meeting room of their dwelling house, but they sat on benches facing each other across the room. They sat on opposite sides of the Meeting House at worship. The Shakers also danced, rolled, or spun wildly during their worship, but men and women didn't touch. Ministers watched through windows to make sure everybody followed the rules.

Come along, then. Let's take a trip back to a damp Saturday in June 1849. A new day is dawning at Pleasant Hill.

The Centre Family Dwelling was constructed of gray stone. Its two center doors provided separate entrances for men and women.

Labor to make the way of God your own;
let it be your inheritance, your treasure,
your occupation, your daily calling.

—Mother Ann

With Benjamin Dunlavy

Brother Benjamin was dreaming of angels. Around and around they danced, in a never-ending wheel. The music they sang sounded sweeter than anything on earth.

Benjamin Dunlavy opened his eyes. Just overhead on the roof of the Centre Family Dwelling, the bell signaled four o'clock in the morning. Through the high windows of the third-floor room, he saw dark treetops silhouetted against a slate gray sky. Time to get up and start another day at Pleasant Hill. The eight young brothers with whom Benjamin shared a room were rising.

As a deacon, one of the leaders of the Centre Family Dwelling, Benjamin wanted to set a good example. Quickly and silently, he slipped out of bed and knelt in prayer. After a few moments, he rose and dressed. Like every other brother, Benjamin put on baggy, gray linen trousers and a loose linen shirt, then slipped on his square-toed shoes. It would be a warm day, so he left his broad-tailed coat hanging on its peg. Carefully, he hung his nightshirt on a high peg. His initials were embroidered inside the nightshirt, as they were inside all his clothes. Sisters would come in later to sweep, tidy, and make the beds. They would wash his nightshirt and hang it back on this peg.

When all were dressed, the eight young brothers formed a line by the door to the hallway. Benjamin stepped to his place at the head of the line. A door across the wide hall opened to show sisters lined up in their room. The sisters wore gray dresses and white bonnets.

Pleasant Hill

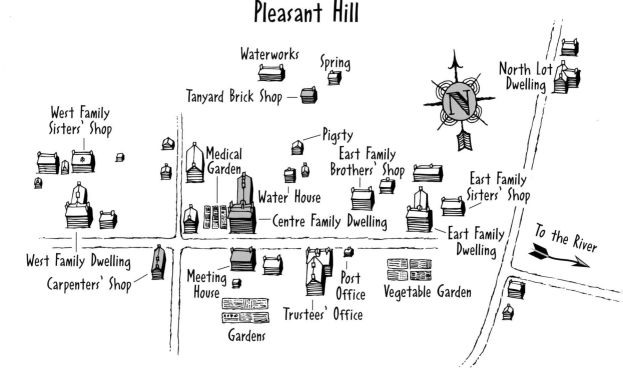

Shaker bedrooms were sparsely furnished with beds, desks, and chairs. Shakers hung their chairs and clothing on wall pegs when they were not using them.

The deaconess, the woman in the doorway, quietly called a greeting. Benjamin called back, careful not to raise his voice. Loud talking indoors was strictly forbidden.

Benjamin turned and looked down the long hall. As soon as the deacon and the deaconess from each sleeping room had appeared in an open doorway, Benjamin stepped forward and nodded. Silently, the brothers marched from their rooms, keeping to their side of the hallway. The women lined up on the other side. Then the men and women descended on separate long, narrow staircases. As they walked, the groups were joined by men and women who slept on the second floor of the Centre Family Dwelling.

People nodded and smiled to each other, but no one spoke. Morning was the time for quiet thought and prayer. Everyone knew exactly what he or she was supposed to do, so there was no need to talk. Life at Pleasant Hill was so carefully patterned that Benjamin found he could move through his days almost without thought.

The line of straight-backed men walked in a stately march down the long stairway. The women did the same on their side. With heads bowed and hands folded in front of them, they filed into the large central hall of the first floor. They turned their faces to the doorways—east for men, west for women—and stepped out onto the stone stoop at the front of the building.

Many Shakers walked out onto the village's main dirt road, muddy after recent rains. Some turned aside to a stone walkway beside the street. Better to keep their shoes clean now than to scrub dirty floors later. When Benjamin stepped outside, the sun was just rising. It was a cool June morning. Heavy clouds gathered in the west. Likely

Shakers filed quietly down the two staircases from the third floor, through the second floor landing (right), *to the main floor.*

it would rain again soon after breakfast. Benjamin glanced at the hand-chiseled, limestone splash blocks. They lay on the ground beneath long pipes, which funneled water from gutters along the high roof. During rainstorms the water cascaded down and hit the splash blocks. They channeled water away from the foundation so that water wouldn't seep into the storage cellars under the house.

Benjamin gazed across the street at the stately, white Meeting House. The building seemed to almost glow in the early morning mist. On the Sabbath (Sunday, the holy day of the week to the Shakers), worship took place in the large room that made up most of the first level.

Benjamin recalled helping to build the Meeting House. The men had labored for ten months, hardly raising their voices or making any unnecessary noise. Sometimes they had carved numbers on the beams. Using the numbers as guides, the builders assembled the giant hand-cut beams on the ground to make sure joints fit together perfectly.

The creative mind behind most of the buildings at Pleasant Hill was Micajah Burnett. In 1809, when Micajah was seventeen, he came with his parents into the Pleasant Hill society. The Shakers sent him to school to study engineering and architecture. By age twenty-three, he had returned to Pleasant Hill. Between 1819 and 1834, Burnett completely changed the layout of the village. He designed family dwellings, barns, mills, shops, offices, and the new Meeting House. Many still stand in perfect condition in modern times. Made from handmade brick, native limestone, and local hardwood, the buildings show the Shaker belief in order and simplicity.

Shakers came together to build the Meeting House, the hub of church and social activity in the village.

Then the builders disassembled the beams and raised them into place with ropes and pulleys.

The ministry lived on the second story of the Meeting House. Benjamin was awed by these holy, solitary leaders. How lonely their lives must be, he often thought. They lived apart from the rest of the village. They neither led nor attended worship services—at least not in the usual way.

On the gentle breeze, Benjamin detected the rancid odor of rotting meat. The smell wafted from the **tanyard** just over the hill, by the creek. His stomach churned when he recalled the times he'd spent working there. Tanning animal hides into leather was necessary to make belts and boots for people and harnesses, reins, and saddles for the horses. Still, it was a horribly smelly business. That's why the tanyard shop was a good half-mile away. That work had made him grateful to the elders for starting the rotation system. Even the nastiest job lasted only a short time. This month Benjamin was assigned to the chair-making shop. That craft was a particular favorite of his.

He hurried on to the wood shop, passing men and women streaming from their dwelling houses. Brothers and sisters headed for red or yellow buildings, sheds, and barns all around the village.

Benjamin walked up the street and turned onto a path to a small, red frame building—the wood shop. Inside, he carefully arranged the tools he would use to cut and shape the wood

Shakers used certain colors for every type of building and shop. Each color had a meaning. The outside of the Meeting House was white, and its interior was trimmed in blue. Both colors suggested purity and holiness to Shakers. The trim in the Meeting House suggested "the sacred blue vault of Heaven" and "the holy waters of life." Wooden buildings nearest the main roads were an attractive, inviting yellow. To Shakers, yellow suggested "the streets of gold" in heaven. Shops and workrooms were painted "workshop red."

Red color came from Kentucky clay, which Shakers dug from the ground. Using this color for shops showed that while the work was important, it was of earthly, not eternal, importance.

he'd use to make a chair. He loved the smell and feel of fresh wood. And creating simple, functional Shaker designs pleased him. So what if the world's people preferred ornate, decorative furniture. Pleasant Hill didn't sell much furniture to the world. Most of the chairs he made furnished the dwelling houses and shops.

The thought of the day's work ahead filled Benjamin with intense joy. He broke into wordless song. Benjamin was lost in his work when the bell sounded again. It was seven o'clock, time for everyone to return to his or her dwelling house for breakfast. Benjamin returned to his room in the Centre Family Dwelling. There he sat quietly for a period of rest. Ten minutes later, in the first floor hallway again, the residents divided into several groups. The dining room wasn't large enough for the whole family to eat at the same time. Benjamin was in the first group to eat this month. The group walked in perfect order through two doors into the dining room.

Serving sisters had already taken the chairs down from their pegs and arranged them around the tables. Benjamin moved to his seat and pulled out the low-backed chair, being careful not to scuff the polished plank floor. He knelt, touching the floor with his right knee first, and prayed silently. Then he rose and settled into his seat. Sisters on kitchen duty carried in steaming bowls of food.

The fourteen brothers who sat at the long plank table with Benjamin quietly passed wooden bowls filled with stewed apples, eggs, and grits. Platters piled with chicken, fresh fruit, and huge biscuits came next. Kitchen sisters appeared with bowls of freshly churned butter, jars of honey, fresh strawberry preserves, and maple syrup.

The house was made of native hardwood and limestone called Kentucky marble. The durable local stone could be cut and polished in the same way as more expensive marble was. The serving sisters bustled in and out of a door that led to the large kitchens at the rear of the building.

Above the door was a huge sunburst window. As he did every morning, Benjamin reflected that the window served no real purpose. And Shakers did not believe in mere decoration. Still, its elegant beauty made him oddly happy—perhaps this was purpose enough.

As Benjamin wiped up his last bit of egg with a biscuit, Sister Patsy approached with more food. He waved her away with a grateful smile. "Shaker your plate" was one of the first lessons he'd learned as a child. "Take as much as you want, but eat everything."

Back in the wood shop, Benjamin went to work. At noon the bell on top of the Centre Family Dwelling would call them all back for a short meal and rest. At five thirty, it would sing them home to evening meal.

Singing softly, Benjamin studied the array of tools hanging from pegs on the wall and lying in neat rows on the workbenches below. He selected a handsaw and carefully began to cut a piece of wood that he'd rounded on a hand lathe the day before. Bent over his work, he felt the same joy and peace he felt during worship. To do a job haphazardly or carelessly wasn't the Shaker way.

In modern times, Shaker furniture is highly prized. One Shaker chair recently sold for over $500,000. What was so special about the chairs the Shakers built? One craftsperson, always male, built each chair. Shakers didn't use the assembly-line method. That would take away the personal touch each carpenter put into his work. A Shaker craftsman could spend weeks making a single chair. He selected just the right wood, cut the pieces, fit them together, sanded them, and applied a finish. He never took shortcuts. Only when every joint and angle was perfect did he feel the piece was complete.

Women prepared the meals at Pleasant Hill. The kitchen was stocked with homegrown vegetables, fresh meats, and dairy products.

Shaking into liberty and life
and simple freedom . . . .
—from a South Union Village hymn, 1854

With Patsy Roberts Williamson

Patsy dried her hands on a towel, sighed, and looked around the large, tidy kitchen. As kitchen deaconess of the Centre Family Dwelling, it was her job to make sure everything ran smoothly. Sisters bustled about, singing and laughing, stacking dirty dishes, and cleaning pots and pans. A young girl bent to scrape breakfast leftovers into a slop bucket. She would feed the scraps to the pigs.

It was barely eight o'clock, yet it would soon be time to begin preparing the noonday meal. Apples left over from breakfast would fill about five pie shells to make a tasty treat for lunch. A girl already stood at the sturdy table in the middle of the room. Patsy watched her as she used a double rolling pin, which had two side-by-side rollers attached to one handle. The girl rolled out dough for the pie shells. Other girls and women carried kindling to stoke the wood-burning ovens, where they would soon bake bread. Sister Patsy instructed two other girls to go to the fowl yard to help Sister Margaret select, kill, and pluck a dozen plump chickens. Roasted chicken was on the menu for supper tonight.

When preparations for the next meal were under way, Patsy made her way up the long, narrow staircase leading from the kitchen to the infirmary just above. She paused to chat with Sister Polly, who was infirmary caretaker for that month. Patsy leaned inside an open door to greet Sarah and Lucy, two elderly sisters who lived in one room of the infirmary.

Sister Patsy waved farewell and stepped down a short hallway, through a low doorway, and into the central meeting room. This wide, airy room with high windows on each side and benches lining the walls was one of Patsy's favorite places. Here on Mondays and Thursdays,

Shakers met inside the Meeting House for social events and worship.

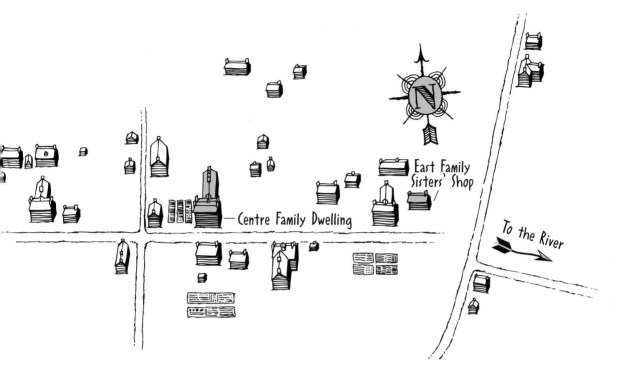

East Family Sisters' Shop

Centre Family Dwelling

To the River

the sisters met to talk, play games, and practice the dances performed in Sunday worship. Tuesdays and Fridays, the brothers met here to relax and rehearse the dances. And on Wednesdays and Saturdays, the brothers and sisters often met to discuss the news of the day, read aloud, or simply sit and chat. Men sat on one side of the room and women on the other.

Patsy stepped into the upstairs hallway. A few sisters were cleaning the sleeping rooms, airing out bedclothes, and gathering laundry to be taken to the washhouse. Patsy loved this time of day between breakfast and their midday meal. Almost everyone was working in the fields and shops. She'd been on her feet since four in the morning, so she looked forward to sitting quietly.

Patsy went into the room she shared with six others

Shakers kept detailed journals and accounts of everyday activities. In their journals, Shakers tracked weather, growing trends, animal breeding records, sales figures, and other village statistics. The journals gave the Shakers a sense of order, growth, and progress. At the end of each year, Shakers could read through their journals to see exactly what they'd accomplished and what still needed to be done.

and shut the door. On a desk lay a sheaf of papers tied with yarn—her journal. Patsy sat down and opened it gently. She read over the past few weeks' entries. Most were about the weather and the business of the kitchen. She had written about the gardens, what flourished and what did not. Patsy smiled as she noticed how many references related to strawberries. The red berries had been plentiful that spring. Women and girls had been busy night and day picking, cleaning, mashing, cooking, and preserving the strawberries in glass jars. Reading it over in her journal, Patsy realized how much they had accomplished. The jam would last for many months.

Patsy picked up her quill pen and dipped the metal tip into a bottle of black ink. She noted the date, then she made a few short notes about the recent cool, rainy weather and the morning's menu. Patsy marveled at her own ability to read and write. Patsy could recall a time when those skills would have been unthinkable.

When she first came to Pleasant Hill in the fall of 1812, Patsy was an 18-year-old slave. She'd come with her owners, Katherine and James Williamson, to join the Society of Believers. Life at Pleasant Hill was like a dream

In a Centre Family Dwelling bedroom, rows of beds with white bedspreads are clean and orderly.

come true for Patsy. Work at Pleasant Hill wasn't numbing drudgery. It was wonderful and fulfilling, because everyone worked together.

Patsy had taught other sisters what she knew about weaving and basketry (basket making). And they taught her how to read and write—something no slave Patsy knew could do. During the worship services, she joined in the ecstatic whirling dances. Songs flowed out of her. And at worship, Patsy was amazed and thrilled to hear her own songs spilling from the lips of others.

A year after she'd arrived, the Williamsons left to return to their former lives. They left word that their slaves, including Patsy, were to follow them. Patsy was crushed, although her Shaker brothers and sisters comforted her as best they could. The afternoon she was preparing to leave with the other Williamson slaves, Elder Samuel Turner and Eldress Anna Cole came to see Patsy at the Centre Family Dwelling. Their mysterious smiles puzzled her until they told her the news. They'd asked the Williamsons to sell Patsy to the Shakers. The Williamsons had agreed! Patsy was free to stay or to go anywhere she wanted.

As she thought again of that glorious day, words of

thanksgiving welled inside her. Quickly, she dipped her pen point into the ink again. She began to write furiously.

After a time, Patsy shut her journal and pushed back her chair. Soon it would be time to return to the kitchen. First, however, she wanted to visit the silk room, where a batch of silkworms had hatched a few weeks before.

Patsy left the Centre Family Dwelling by the side door. Rain was falling lightly, but the clouds were already breaking up to show bright blue sky. She hurried across the yard to the square, two-storied weaving shop. She noticed the neat row of mulberry trees as she passed them. Some years ago, Shakers had planted the trees because silkworms ate nothing but mulberry leaves.

Inside the shop, sisters were spinning and weaving. Patsy called a greeting as she mounted the stairs. She was glad to notice that, as always, the temperature rose as she reached the top floor. Silkworms needed warm, still air to flourish. Stoves kept the room at a constant eighty degrees.

Patsy carefully rattled the door before entering, warning the silkworms. The insects were sensitive to noise and movement. Since agitated caterpillars spun poor quality silk, visitors announced their arrival. When she stepped inside the room, Patsy smiled as every silkworm turned toward the door. The silkworms always welcomed visitors this way. The silkworms lived in twenty wide, shallow baskets, which filled the shelves lining the room. Inside each basket were leafy mulberry twigs. Patsy checked to make sure the leaves in the baskets were green and moist. The leaves had to be replaced several times a day because they wilted quickly.

Children collected fresh leaves and lay them in the

Approximately one thousand silkworms lived in each basket. When they were about one month old, they stopped eating and started spinning a silky cocoon. Most cocoons would be placed in the hot sun to kill the silkworm. After the silkworms died, sisters would boil the cocoons in hot, soapy water to remove the sticky substance holding each cocoon together. Then sisters would unravel each cocoon by hand. After she found the end of the thread, a worker carefully unwound it and rolled it onto a spool. Women used a spinning wheel to twist the threads from three or four cocoons into a sturdy fiber. Workers would dye it and weave the fiber on a loom to make beautiful, lustrous fabric. Merchants all over the country sold Shaker silk.

baskets for the little caterpillars to eat. The children also cleaned dried leaves and debris from the baskets, and they made sure that the caterpillars were placed near the new food. The children often treated the little worms like pets—naming them, letting them crawl on their hands and arms, talking to them, and petting them. Patsy was glad to see that the baskets were neat and full of fresh leaves. The children had done their tasks well.

Patsy walked briskly back to the kitchen, where she saw sisters finishing preparations for the noon meal. Patsy walked through the dining room and into the building's long front hallway. She checked the time at a tall clock between the doors. Nearly a quarter to twelve! She hurried back into the kitchen.

She stood on tiptoe to unwind the thick bell rope from its hook on the wall. The rope passed through an opening in the high ceiling. It stretched three stories to the big bell on the roof. When Patsy pulled the rope, the bell tolled high above.

The countryside around Pleasant Hill was dotted with farm buildings in the 1800s.

Little children are nearer the kingdom
of heaven than those a riper older age.
—Mother Ann Lee

With Hortensia Hooser

Across a meadow thick with wet grass, a line of fifteen little girls marched silently. They ranged in age from six to about twelve, and all were members of the East Family's Children's Order. All wore long linen skirts and white cotton bonnets tied with thin ribbons beneath their chins. At the head of the column strode Hortensia Hooser, their teacher and caretaker. She wore a bonnet, too, over her thin, netlike sister's cap. In one hand, Sister Hortensia held a tall walking stick, and under her arm she clutched a thick book. As she marched, Hortensia hummed a marching song. In a nearby field, boys hoed weeds growing between rows of newly sprouted corn.

Soon the group walked along a sandy creek bed. Hortensia paused to point out several trees whose roots made refreshing or medicinal teas. She showed them poisonous plants, such as nightshade and hemlock, which

The *Millennial Laws* was a long list of rules about how Shakers should live and work. "Millennial" refers to a one-thousand-year period. The Shakers believed they were living in the final one thousand years of peace mentioned in the Bible. After that time, Jesus would return and the world would end. The Laws were set down to show Shakers how to live during this final period.

The Laws declared, among other things, that at night everyone should "retire to rest in the fear of God, without any playing or boisterous laughter, and lie straight." When Shakers lined up for meals or to march to and from worship, lines were always to be perfectly straight.

they should never touch. Some of the younger girls began to whine. They thought that school had ended in March.

Sister Hortensia smiled. School only lasted four months each year—not long enough! The girls could learn all year round. She dug into the soft papery wood of a rotting log. The girls gathered around her to examine a fat grub writhing in the wood.

Later they returned to the village. Behind the washhouse, where many sisters were busy with laundry, Sister Hortensia paused. She pointed to three small sheds with slots high up under the eaves—the apiaries, or bee houses. Bees buzzed busily in and out of the slots from dawn to dusk. The bees had all the sweet honeycomb they needed for themselves, with enough left over to share with others. A hive of happy, busy bees— that's what Shakers are, Hortensia told them. With their arms spread and fluttering, buzzing noisily, the group of girls headed off again. They took a wide, arcing path back to the main road.

Back at the East Family Dwelling, the girls sat on the

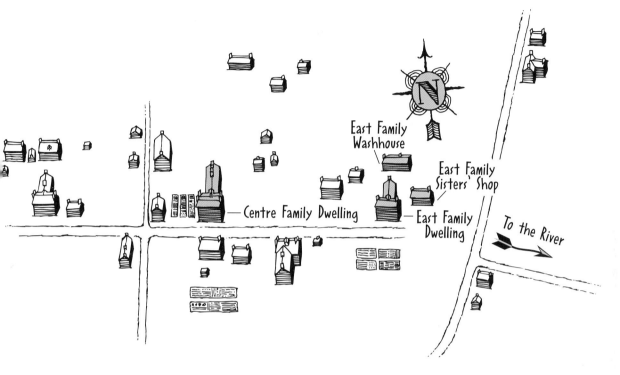

East Family
Washhouse

East Family
Sisters' Shop

Centre Family Dwelling

East Family
Dwelling

To the River

front steps and took off their dirty shoes. Carefully, they lined the shoes in single file on top of the slat fence fronting the house. When the mud on their shoes dried, the girls would brush it off with wads of fresh hay from the stable. They all walked upstairs to the three rooms assigned to them. Each girl took a broom and swept part of the floor. When the room was tidy, the smaller girls lay down on their beds for a short nap. The older girls talked quietly, read, did needlework, or mended garments. Hortensia used the time to make a journal entry.

An hour later, Sister Hortensia and the girls left the house and headed down the road in a jagged line. Several girls would help the kitchen deaconesses of the East and

Shakers invented the sulfur match, the screw propeller for boats, and the first commercial washing machine. There was even a rumor going around that a Shaker was working on a flying machine.

In 1798 a Shaker brother improved the bristle broom that everyone—Shaker or not—used for sweeping. Brother Theodore's broom had tightly fastened bristles that were cut straight across on the bottom. He devised a machine to lace and cut the brooms. After this, Shakers sold thousands of brooms to the world.

Centre Families prepare dinner. Other girls walked to the kitchen and herb gardens to clear dead plants and to yank up fast-growing weeds. Soon the gardeners would plant new tomato and potato plants.

Sister Hortensia took five girls to a spinning shop, where sisters used spinning wheels to transform wool into yarn. The girls sat in a circle on the floor. A pile of coarse wool lay in the middle of the circle. A sister gave each girl a set of carding paddles—broad, flat squares of wood with sharp spikes embedded in them. The girls would card the wool, or clean and separate the fibers. Hortensia showed them to hold one paddle in each hand. She picked up a wad of matted sheep's wool and showed the girls how to comb and work the wool between the spikes. When the wool was a mass of straight, clean fibers, it was ready for spinning. Satisfied that the girls knew what to do, Hortensia headed back to the East House for a short rest.

The girls carded and carded until their arms ached.

But gradually the knotted, dirty wool turned into fluffy gray balls. They set the carded wool in a basket and rested their arms while Sister Polly and Sister Martha took handfuls of the carded wool. It was ready to spin into yarn. They showed the girls how to hold the carded wool in one hand and pull out a few fibers at a time. The spinning wheel pulled the fibers through a small opening and twisted them together. The finished yarn wound itself around a bobbin (a large spool). The wheel did most of the work. After the demonstration, the girls took their turns. The girls struggled to pump the foot pedal to make the wheel spin at just the right speed and pull out the fibers at the same time.

Five bobbins wound tightly with newly spun yarn lay on the floor next to Sister Martha's spinning wheel. She

Shaker sisters at Pleasant Hill used spinning wheels to turn raw wool into yarn.

asked the girls to carry three of them to the dyer's shop. The other two bobbins should go directly to the weavers.

The girls left the spinning shop and followed stepping stones to the dyer's shop. The girls laid three of the spools of dull, grayish yarn on a table. Sisters would dip the yarn into a deep, steaming vat of indigo (dark blue) dye.

Dyeing was messy, smelly work. The colors spattered the sisters' clothes and skin. It was always easy to tell who was working in the dyer's shop—their stained hands and arms gave them away. Long, dripping strands of newly dyed yarn hung from the drying racks. When the yarn had dried, two sisters took it off the racks and wound it onto spools.

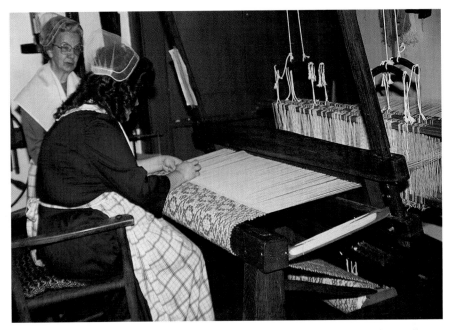

Weavers created soft, luxurious fabrics from silk thread. Shaker silk was well known and desired all over the country.

It was easy to lose track of time watching the dyers at work. But the girls had to bring the rest of the yarn to the weavers. They crossed to the shop just next door. Inside the weaving shop, the girls passed shelves stacked with spools and spools of dyed and undyed yarns.

Two sisters were busy at looms made of heavy wooden beams. The sisters' nimble fingers held a wooden shuttle attached to a long piece of yarn. The sisters passed the shuttle back and forth between the raised **warp threads.** The beater thumped, and another line of fabric was complete. By repeating the procedure several thousand times, a weaver created a piece of fabric.

As the sisters wove, yard after yard of woolen cloth appeared on a beam (roll). Beams of checkered, striped, and plain cotton and wool cloth hung on racks around the walls. Sisters in the dressmaking and tailoring shops would use the cloth to make dresses, pants, shirts, and coats—everything that people wore at Pleasant Hill. They also made sheets, blankets, and carpeting.

Gazing at the sisters' busy fingers, the girls didn't notice time passing. A gentle voice behind them broke their spell. They turned to see Sister Hortensia standing by the door. The rest of the girls waited outside.

They lined up behind Sister Hortensia and marched back to the East Family Dwelling. The girls would practice reading and arithmetic for the rest of the afternoon. Hortensia used her walking stick to point at trees as they passed. She asked the girls the name of each tree, what the bark was good for, if the leaves were edible. And on and on. For Sister Hortensia, the world was one big classroom. She never let her young students forget it.

Next to the Centre Family Dwelling, doctors grew plants and flowers to use in homemade medicines. Shakers also dried them for potpourri.

But as the science of prevention
Far surpasses that of cure
To it you should pay more attention
By which a blessing you'll secure.

—John Shain, *To My Successor in the Medical Profession*

With John Shain

John Shain walked among the rows of his medical garden next to the Centre Family Dwelling. This small garden was separate from the nearby kitchen garden, where sisters raised tasty plants used for spicing up food. The plants in John's medical garden would be used in medicines he prepared himself.

Though it was only June, dozens of plants were well established. He'd have a fine selection of herbs to choose from in another month. John absently bent to pull insect eggs and dead leaves from plants as he moved along. Two sisters picking peas in the nearby kitchen garden called to him cheerfully. Deep in thought, John did not respond. Worry lines creased his thin face.

A terrible **cholera** epidemic (outbreak) raged in the countryside. Every day, the Pleasant Hill Shakers got word of more deaths in Lexington and on surrounding farms. More than forty people in Harrodsburg, only seven miles away, had already died. Shakers had discussed suspending meetings in the Meeting House until the epidemic subsided. As yet, though, no one at Pleasant Hill had fallen ill with the horrible disease.

More and more lately, John felt an awesome responsibility as the community's only physician. The Shakers depended on him to heal cuts, bruises, scrapes, and scratches, as well as to ease sore throats, colds, headaches, coughs, and rheumatism. John used teas, salves, plasters, **poultices,** and pills to heal these injuries and illnesses. But he worried about the diseases that could spread like wildfire in dry grass. Measles, scarlet fever, tuberculosis, and now cholera!

Although no one knew for certain how these diseases spread, John believed that poor living conditions must be partly responsible. People were generally healthy at Pleasant Hill. John thought he knew why—they enjoyed sunlight, exercise, fresh air, hard work, clean water, and wholesome food. John knew that people in surrounding villages ate fatty, salt-cured meats and few fresh

Pleasant Hill Shakers grew and dried hundreds of varieties of medicinal plants and flowers. The Shakers were the first people in America to grow herbs on a large scale to be sold as medicines. Beginning about 1820 and continuing for the rest of the century, people swore by Shaker dried herbs, extracts, herbal oils, and concentrated pills. Few other remedies and drugs seemed reliable. Shakers were noted for their cleanliness and honesty in all matters, so people assumed—rightly—that Shaker medicines would be good.

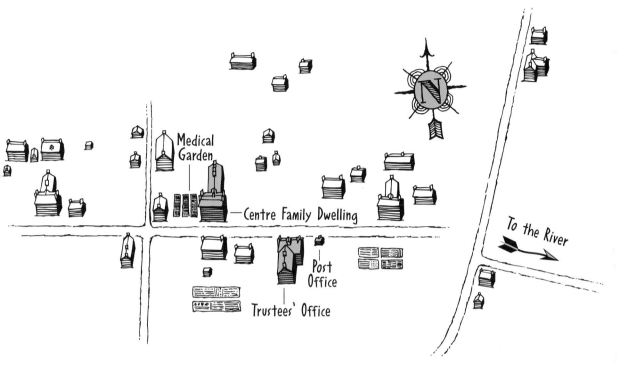

Medical Garden

Centre Family Dwelling

Post Office

Trustees' Office

To the River

fruits or vegetables. Runoff from toilets or barn lots polluted their wells and cisterns (tanks for water storage). And their filthy, airless cabins made a sharp contrast to the tidy Shaker dwellings.

John sighed heavily and straightened. He set off down the road toward the Trustees' Office. He knew he would find Elder Micajah Burnett there.

Just down from the Centre Family Dwelling, John paused to look at the Trustees' Office. The three-storied, red-brick building had six tall chimneys towering above its tiled roof. Although the Trustees' Office was one of the village's most ornate structures, its purpose was purely functional. The building combined the functions of a

The brick Trustees' Office housed offices for Shaker leaders.

business office, hotel, dining room, and home for a few of the older members of the community.

John walked to stone steps leading up to the impressive front door. It had two side windows and a brass doorknob and lock. John looked up, as he always did, at the semicircular, sunburst window over the door.

John pushed the latch on the front door and stepped inside. He stood in a long narrow hallway that ran back to the dining area and kitchen. Smaller offices and rooms lined the hallway. He walked to the foot of the men's staircase. It had a glistening cherry wood rail. He tilted his head far back and looked up. The staircase curved gracefully to the top floor, and it was lit from above by skylights.

Elder Micajah Burnett, the man John had come to see, had designed the Trustees' Office and its staircases. As John's designated confessor, Elder Micajah listened as John confessed his sins and weaknesses each week. But John hadn't come today to confess. He needed something else—reassurance.

John walked down a long hallway to a door, on which he gently tapped. At a call from within, he opened the door and went inside. Sitting at a desk stacked with papers and drawings was Elder Micajah Burnett. The elder looked up at John and smiled, then got up to clear books and papers from a chair so that John could sit.

The staircase inside the Trustees' Office is freestanding, with clean lines and graceful curves. A skylight in the roof lights each staircase.

John told him that the cholera epidemic seemed to be closing in. Elder Burnett heard him out, letting John express his worries. When John finished speaking, Elder Burnett reassured him. John was one of the most knowledgeable horticulturists in the western United States. He'd written articles for scholarly journals about the healing properties of native Kentucky plants. He could hardly imagine a more capable physician for the community than John Shain. Elder Burnett told John these things in a straightforward manner. As always, Micajah's tone was calm and direct, not flattering. John knew the elder was simply reporting the facts as he saw them.

As John started to go, Micajah caught his sleeve. Sorting mail earlier in the post office, he'd seen a letter addressed to John. In addition to his duties as elder and trustee, Elder Burnett was also the village's postman. Together the men walked next door to the dark red post office. It was the closest village building to the main road. This allowed the stagecoach, which stopped twice a day on its way between Lexington and Harrodsburg, to drive right up to the door. Micajah pulled the large key from his pocket and opened the door.

Inside, Burnett found the letter and handed it to John. He watched John tear open the letter and read. After a moment, John handed him the letter. Micajah's duties included reading every piece of mail that men in his charge received.

The letter was from a lawyer in Bullitt County, sixty miles away. John's niece Nancy Pennebaker and her husband, William, had died of cholera. The letter concluded with Nancy's dying wish that the Shakers adopt her children. The writer requested that John fetch the children, who were staying with neighbors.

John hurried back to the Centre Family Dwelling. As one of the village's traders, John often made trips to distant cities and towns, so he knew how to travel light. It took him only a few minutes to fill his deep cloth satchel with a change of clothes and a few personal items. He left the satchel by the front door of the house and, grabbing a basket, made a quick trip to his medical garden. He bent to pull some tender leaves from tansy, thyme, and peppermint plants and dropped them into his basket.

Carrying his small basket of herbs, he walked to the side door of the dwelling. He walked down the steps to the cool, dark cellar—the storage area for the entire dwelling. John made his way between the stacks of wooden barrels and boxes of every shape and size. In another room, shelves lined the walls from floor to ceiling.

Shaker doctors grew, chopped, and pressed herbs to create medicines.

The shelves supported hundreds of glass jars of preserves, fruits, and vegetables. Casks and barrels filled with flour, wheat, barley, and dried corn filled yet another room.

John opened the door to the herb room and stepped inside. On a low, wide table next to the door lay a lantern and assorted tools. A press that could squeeze juice from green plants and berries was next to knives and a small cleaver for chopping herbs. John opened the small tin lantern and lit the candle inside. He raised the light and examined the dry herbs hanging from racks and ropes all around. Many of these would be packaged and sold to the world when he made his next peddling (selling) trip.

John pulled down some well-dried leaves and dropped them into his basket. He chose several bottles from a shelf, blew out the candle, and stepped to the door. He placed the lantern on the table again. A room down the hall contained hundreds of candles, each hand-dipped by sisters during the long winter. But even so, John didn't want to waste a single drip of this one.

Down the hall, John entered his work area, a room brightly lit by sun shining through the large windows on one side. He chopped the plants he'd collected. Next, John carefully mixed a few herbs in a shallow glass container. Then, he slowly put various amounts of the herbs into four glass mugs. Upstairs in the kitchen, he added boiling water and gently stirred them.

On the second floor, directly above the warm kitchen, six small rooms served as the village hospital and clinic. Two elderly sisters, Lucy and Sarah, shared one room. Nothing ailed them except old age. Sister Polly tended them. In a room across the hall lay Brother William, a young man about twenty years old. He had a broken leg, several broken ribs, and an assortment of scrapes, scratches, and bruises. After a run-in with the village's prize bull, he was lucky to be alive. In another room lay a boy named Andrew, who had a fever and a cough. The men's caretaker, Brother Paul, tended them both.

John stopped in each room to administer the herbs he'd prepared. He paused to inspect a wheelchair he had asked a brother to make for the infirmary. Two small wheels had been added to the front and two large wheels in the back of a simple, slat-backed chair. It would make it much easier for the caretakers to move their patients from room to room.

John gave Brother Paul a poultice made from slippery elm bark and witch hazel. Paul would use it on Brother William to lessen swelling and inflammation. John also gave Brother Paul a syrup. John had dropped in some nails to add iron and had boiled the mixture for three hours. The medicine should help Andrew's cough. John bent over the side of Andrew's bed and gently felt the boy's hot forehead. If the fever hadn't gone away by the time John returned from his trip, he'd try doses of dogwood bark or boneset leaves.

Two hours later, John was jostling in a wagon headed toward the road to Bullitt County. It was growing dark. He would travel all night to reach his destination by noon the next day, Sunday. John knew that the children—Francis, Sarah, and William—would be heartbroken over the loss of their parents. John would do his best to comfort them and to prepare them for the trip back to Pleasant Hill. There, a home and a family of two hundred brothers and sisters would be waiting to embrace them.

The peaceful stream at Pleasant Hill provided the Shakers with clean, fresh water.

My heavenly home is here,
No longer need I wait.

—A Shaker hymn

With a Visitor

A man in a long dark coat and a wide-brimmed black hat shaded his eyes and craned his neck backward. High over his head soared sheer limestone palisades, or cliffs. The stone cliffs stretched for miles along both sides of the Kentucky River valley. The road rose, steep and rocky, to wind through a natural cut in the rock. His mare, Della, arched her neck to drink greedily from the river. The traveler dismounted and stooped to gather a cupped handful of water for himself.

The man in black peered across the river. The water didn't appear too deep, nor did the current seem too rapid. Still, the traveler knew enough not to venture into unknown water. Somewhere along here was a ferryboat. He hoped the ferryman hadn't taken this Sunday morning off. There was no other way to get across the river. He heard a sharp whistle from across the river. A man stood on the shore waving his arms. The traveler waved back. The man disappeared among the thick willows. In a moment, he appeared poling a long, flat ferryboat.

The traveler and his horse waited patiently for the ferryman. In a few moments, the man in black led Della aboard the ferry. The ferryman leaned against his long pole to shove the boat toward the other shore. The traveler held tight to Della's bridle as she fidgeted nervously, not liking the sight of land receding behind her. The ferryman wiped sweat from his brow and smiled. The traveler said he was a lawyer, taking a few days off to see a Shaker worship service.

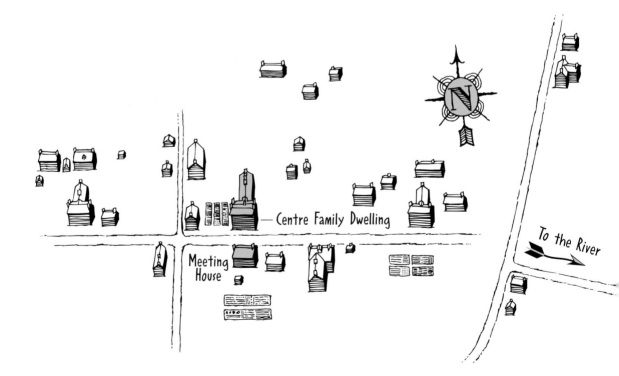

The ferryboat operator made a sweeping motion with his callused hand to indicate the extent of the Shaker lands. His gesture took in the opposite shore and the land immediately atop the high palisades. The traveler could make out several long frame buildings on stone foundations, just a few yards from the water's edge. The ferryman said that they were full of goods waiting for steamboats to take them downriver to Louisville, Kentucky, and then to New Orleans, Louisiana.

The traveler led his horse ashore. He mounted, then turned and tossed the ferry operator a fifty-cent piece. The ferryman caught it and touched the brim of his hat. He called a farewell as the traveler started up the narrow winding road toward Pleasant Hill.

He found the upward trek thrilling. The winding, turning road seemed little more than a shelf of stone cut into the limestone cliff. The view of the river valley and palisades was stunning.

When the road widened, they left the rocky ledge behind. The traveler found himself surrounded by wide, tree-lined meadows. In the distance, he could make out hills already green with flax and corn. Stone walls, skillfully constructed of stacked rocks, ran along the road and into the fields, separating grazing cattle and sheep from grainfields.

In a moment, the man became aware of sound. An airy, rushing roar, it rose and fell like the sound of the sea. Della heard it, too, and tossed her head and nickered. A mile across the rolling fields, the visitor could see the top of a tall building. A small cupola (a rounded structure on top of a building) stood out against the sky. The visitor realized that the sound was of many voices, a hundred or more, lifted in song. He had read that Shaker worship could often be heard from a great distance. Now he knew it was true.

His pocket watch said it was almost one in the afternoon. The traveler tapped Della's sides with his heels to hurry her toward Pleasant Hill. When the man arrived in the village, he found that he was not the only visitor that Sunday afternoon. Carriages, wagons, and horses lined the main street. Families picnicked under trees. Couples strolled arm in arm, pointing at the stately stone buildings. A crowd stood before the Meeting House, the place he'd come to visit.

The visitor tied Della in the shade of a large tree and began to step through the crowd toward the front of the Meeting House. He opened the door and stepped inside, removing his hat. He saw a huge room that reminded him

At the Meeting House, Shakers welcomed visitors who came to observe their Sunday worship.

of a great hall, but he saw no preacher and heard no sermon. The room was almost silent. About fifty to seventy-five men sat on long benches on one side of the room. Across the hall, an equal number of women sat on benches facing them. He saw no children. Each head was bowed, as if in prayer, each person's hands tightly clasped. A thin bench, lined with finely dressed visitors, ran along all four walls. He found a small gap next to a bearded man holding a stovepipe hat and sat down.

The visitor noted that black and white Shakers sat side-by-side. In 1849 such unity of the races was extremely rare. There was a stirring among the female members, then a middle-aged woman stood and began to speak. Every face turned toward the speaker. The woman talked softly but confidently as she said how happy she was to be a Shaker. A dozen others rose to speak after her. Each expressed joy and contentment to be a member of Pleasant Hill.

At some unseen signal, the whole company stood. Their voices rose in perfect unison and they sang a hymn. As the voices rose in volume, the man was sure that the walls of the building were quaking. Then the voices sounded soft and airy.

The visitor saw the Shakers pick up and move the benches, which they stacked neatly against the wall, leaving the wide floor completely empty. Stepping solemnly, the Shakers began to march.

One song ended and another began, then another and another, each with a different tone, rhythm, and message. The dance shifted as the orderly rows became circles of men and circles of women. Although the circles intertwined,

Shakers thought no handmade instrument could improve upon the God-given one—the human voice. They sang without musical accompaniment. Some hymns didn't have words either. Shakers performed these by singing "la," "lo," or other syllables in place of words. In other cases, singers used their voices to imitate the sounds of musical instruments. A few hymns weren't in the words of a known language. The Shakers said that these were written in "angel tongues" received from supernatural sources.

they never touched. Eventually the whole group whirled together in six huge, moving circles. Each circle rotated in a different direction from the one adjacent to it. The singing grew more intense and insistent. The faces of the Shakers glowed, as if lit from within.

Suddenly each dancer whirled apart from the others. Worshipers threw back their heads and waved their hands, legs, and arms in all directions. Songs mingled with screams, shouts, grunts, and groans. Some dancers fell to the floor and writhed. They resembled people in a fit, in horrible pain, or overwhelmed by joy. Some wept. Others laughed. Still others spoke loudly in some unknown language.

The visitor looked up and found a male face peering at him through a small window high on the wall on the west side of the building. He turned and found another window on the east end of the room, this one with a female in it. Ministers were keeping an eye on the worship.

The wild ceremony lasted into the afternoon. Watchers rose and left. Others took their places. The dark-clad visitor found himself unable to break free from the spirit of the place. He sat spellbound, drinking in every sound and motion.

Men and women marched separately during worship services.

After a while, he felt a hand on his shoulder. He looked up and found a kind-faced older man smiling at him. The Shaker gently motioned for the visitor to follow. The traveler rose and followed the old man out of the Meeting House.

Outside, most other visitors had gone home. The traveler and the old Shaker slowly walked along. The elder answered the visitor's questions. After a time, the two men stood in silence. The minister fixed a steady gaze on the visitor. The lawyer was deep in thought. Just down the street, Della had spotted her master. She gave a loud nicker, but he didn't seem to be aware of her. The men walked into one of the houses as a bell sounded overhead. Soon the street was empty, except for a line of white ducks, waddling their way to a still lake that reflected a gold and crimson sunset.

Near dusk, a boy came and untied Della's reins from the tree. He spoke in soothing tones, patting her side. He led her to a barn filled with many other horses, munching sweet hay. They neighed and stamped a greeting.

When the Civil War came to Kentucky, the Union and the Confederate armies fought battles close to Pleasant Hill.

Times have changed and the world moves forward.

—Emma King, a Shaker minister

Afterword

When the Civil War began in 1861, the Shakers refused to fight. Though they hated slavery and believed the Union should not be destroyed, Shakers were still pacifists. They would take no part in the war. However, their neighbors looked on them with anger and suspicion.

Still, the Union army made it clear—if Shaker men wouldn't volunteer, they would be forced to fight. In 1862 a committee of Shakers went to the nation's capital in Washington, D.C., to plead with President Lincoln to officially excuse their men from military duty. Mr. Lincoln expressed his disappointment that Shakers didn't want to help their country. Yet he understood their moral dilemma and signed an order releasing all Shaker men from military responsibility.

Even so, the Shakers couldn't stay isolated from the

Civil War. In October 1862, Pleasant Hill found itself at the crossroads of the most vicious battle fought in Kentucky. At Perryville, a small village only twenty miles away, the Confederate and Union armies met in a three-day clash. The Shakers set up hospitals and treated wounded and dying soldiers, both Confederate and Union.

Gunfire and the roar of cannons could be clearly heard from Pleasant Hill. Soldiers charged back and forth through the village. Starving soldiers flocked to the village, begging for food at every window and door. Sisters cooked and baked day and night trying to keep up with the demand. They set up tables along the road and kept them filled with food. One day alone, they fed over 1,400 soldiers. The Shakers never turned away anyone who asked for help.

When the Battle of Perryville was over and the armies moved to fight in other places, the Shakers were left with empty storerooms. They had barely enough left to feed themselves for the coming winter. The Civil War spelled the beginning of the end for the Shakers at Pleasant Hill. When the war was finally over in 1865, the Shakers' Southern markets for goods were gone. No one had money to buy Shaker products, no matter how good.

As a new century dawned, the Industrial Revolution lured people away from hard farmwork. State institutions for the care of orphans meant fewer young orphans were left in Shaker care. And, of course, Shakers could not marry and have children on their own.

In 1896 about sixty Shakers lived at Pleasant Hill. By 1910 only twelve elderly sisters remained. Nearly all of the buildings and barns had fallen into decay. The shining white Meeting House stood silent. The 1,800 remaining acres of Pleasant Hill were covered in weeds and thistle.

In desperation, the elderly sisters gave the land to a local farmer. He promised to take care of them for their remaining years. The last Shaker at Pleasant Hill, Mary Settles, died in 1923. All the buildings and their contents were auctioned off. The Meeting House became an auto mechanic's shop. Other buildings became stores, gas stations, warehouses, and private homes. Many simply fell into ruin from neglect. It seemed a sad end for such a peaceful, vital place.

Over the years, people still visited Pleasant Hill to remember how it used to be. Visitors tried to recall the happy, industrious people who had once lived and worked in the stately buildings. A group formed to rescue Pleasant Hill for future generations.

In 1960 the group began to purchase and restore the site building by building. Shaker furniture, tools, and

At a Pleasant Hill workshop, a modern-day interpreter makes famous Shaker boxes according to Shaker methods.

Costumed interpreters serve typical Shaker meals to visitors. Tourists can feel how it was to be a Shaker at Pleasant Hill.

items of every sort were discovered in the structures' basements and attics. In the 1970s, the state of Kentucky opened Pleasant Hill Village as a living museum.

In modern times, 33 of the original 270 structures stand on 2,800 acres. Experts have taken great care to make each house and shop look the way it did in 1850. Ongoing studies of the grounds, fields, and gardens reveal new things about how the Shakers of Pleasant Hill lived and worked.

Interpreters in costumes kindly welcome visitors and tell them about the Shakers. Workers serve delicious Shaker food in the dining halls. Gardens grow from seeds carefully preserved by Shaker hands. Old looms once again produce beautiful fabrics, and shops turn out oval boxes, baskets, and butter churns. Hymns and laughter ring out again in the Meeting House. People flock to see the old dances performed. In this way, the Shakers seem very much alive at Pleasant Hill.

Glossary

cholera: An often-fatal disease caused by bacteria.

elder: A leader in the Shaker community. Elders assigned tasks and monitored resources in Shaker villages. They also served as spiritual advisers to members of their villages.

family: A group sharing a communal dwelling in a Shaker village. Each family at Pleasant Hill had about one hundred male and female members. Each family also had its own elders.

ministry: The highest local authority in a Shaker village. The men and women of the ministry lived apart from the rest of the village and oversaw all aspects of village life.

poultice: A soft medicinal lotion spread on a cloth that is applied to sores and scrapes.

tanyard: An area containing vats of chemicals used for tanning animal hides to make them into leather.

warp thread: The yarn stretched vertically on a weaving loom, across which a yarn is horizontally woven to create cloth.

the world: Anything outside of the Shaker villages. Shakers referred to non-Shakers as **the world's people.**

Pronunciation Guide

cholera	KAH-luh-ruh
dissenters	dih-SEHN-tuhrz
herbalist	UHR-buh-lihst
infirmary	ihn-FUHRM-ree
lathe	LAYTH
poultice	POHL-tuhs

Further Reading

Archambeault, James. *The Gift of Pleasant Hill: Shaker Community in Kentucky.* Harrodsburg, KY: Pleasant Hill Press, 1991.

Bial, Raymond. *Shaker Home.* Boston: Houghton Mifflin, 1994.

Bolick, Nancy O'Keefe, and Sallie G. Randolph. *Shaker Villages.* New York: Walker and Company, 1993.

Gaeddert, LouAnn. *Hope.* New York: Atheneum Books for Young Readers, 1995.

Ray, Mary Lyn. *Shaker Boy.* San Diego: Browndeer Press, 1994.

Turner, Ann Warren. *Shaker Hearts.* New York: HarperCollins Publishers, 1997.

Williams, Jean Kinney. *The Shakers.* New York: Franklin Watts, 1997.

Touring Information

Shaker Village of Pleasant Hill is open for touring every day of the year except December 24 and 25. Touring hours are from 9:30 A.M. to 5:30 P.M., April through October. Winter hours may vary. Village tour tickets are sold until 4:30 P.M. For more information,

write to:
Shaker Village of Pleasant Hill
3501 Lexington Road
Harrodsburg, Kentucky 40330

or call:
(800) 734-5611 or (606) 734-5411

or visit the website at:
<http://www.shakervillageky.org>

Index

brooms, 33–34
Bullitt County, 47
Burnett, Micajah, 17, 43–44

Centre Family Dwelling, 9,
    12–13, 15, 20–21, 23, 27–28,
    38, 41, 45
cholera, 40, 44
Civil War, 56–58

deacons, 10, 13

East Family Dwelling, 33, 37
East Family's Children's
    Order, 31
East House, 35
elders, 7–8, 10

gardens, 26, 34, 38–39, 45

herb room, 46
hospital and clinic
    (infirmary), 24, 46–47
hymns, 53–54

Industrial Revolution, 58
infirmary (hospital and
    clinic), 24

journals, 26, 28, 33

kitchen, 23, 26, 29, 34

Lees, Ann (Mother Ann), 5–7
Lincoln, Abraham, 57
Louisville, Kentucky, 51

Manchester, England, 5
medicines, 38–40
Meeting House, 9, 17–19, 40,
    52, 58–60
ministers, 10–11, 18, 54

New Lebanon, New York, 8
New Orleans, Louisiana, 51
Niskeyuna, New York
    (Watervliet), 6–7, 9

Perryville, Battle of, 58
Pleasant Hill, founding of, 8–9
post office, 44

Revolutionary War, 7

silk room, 28–29
silk thread, 36–37
sleeping rooms, 25–27
spinning, 28, 34–37

tanyard, 18–19
trustees, 10
Trustees' Office, 41–44

United Society of Believers in
    Christ's Second Appearing
    (Shakers), 5
Union army, 56–58

washhouse, 25, 32
weaving, 27–28, 36-37
wood shop, 19, 21
worship services, 4, 27, 52–53

About the Author

Michael Capek has warm memories of trips his family took to Pleasant Hill when he was a boy. "Pleasant Hill was always a fun and exciting trip, even though many of the buildings hadn't yet been restored. It didn't matter. I sensed there was a story behind every hill and tree. I could hear something whispered in the walls of the meetinghouse, and hear something singing in the voice of the old bell atop the Centre Family Dwelling. Now I know it was saying, 'This is what human beings can accomplish if they will only work together for a common cause and treat each other with love and respect.' "

A retired teacher and native Kentuckian, Capek is the author of other books for Lerner Publications Company, including *Artistic Trickery: The Tradition of Trompe L'Oeil Art; Murals: Cave, Cathedral, to Street;* and *Globe-trotters Club: Jamaica.* He also writes educational material used in schools throughout the country. His stories and articles appear in many popular children's magazines.

Acknowledgments

For quoted material: p. 5, *Millenial Praises, containing a collection of Gospel Hymns, in four parts* (Hancock, MA: Josiah Tallcott, Jr., 1813), microfiche; p. 13, Kathleen Mahoney, *Simple Wisdom: Shaker Sayings, Poems, and Songs* (New York: Penguin Books, 1993); p. 23, Benjamin Dunlavy, "Shaking into Liberty and Life," songbook (Lebanon, OH: Warren County Historical Society, n.d.); p. 31, Calvin Green and Seth Y. Wells, eds., *Testimonies Concerning the Character and Ministry of Mother Ann Lee and the First Witnesses of the Gospel of Christ's Second Appearing: Given by Some of the Aged Brethren and Sisters of the United Society, Including a Few Sketches of their Own Appearance* (Albany, NY: Packard and Benthuysen, 1827) microfiche; p. 49: June Spring, *By Shaker Hands* (New York: Alfred A. Knopf, 1975); p. 57, Emma B. King, *A Shaker's Viewpoint* (Old Chatham, NY: Shaker Museum Foundation, 1957).

For photos and artwork: Shaker Village of Pleasant Hill, KY, pp. 1, 9, 22, 24, 35, 45; North Wind Picture Archives, pp. 4, 10, 18; Brown Brothers, pp. 7, 55; © Andre Jenny/Unicorn Stock Photos, p. 12, © Paul Murphy/Unicorn Stock Photos, pp. 15, 16, 34; © Kay Shaw, pp. 27, 36, 42; © Robin Rudd/Unicorn Stock Photos, p. 30; © Buddy Mays/Travel Stock, pp. 38, 43, 52; © Jeff Rogers/Shaker Village of Pleasant Hill, KY, pp. 48, 59, 60; The Filson Club, p. 56. Cover photograph courtesy of: © Kay Shaw.